Excellence in Supervision
Essential Skills for the New Supervisor

Rick Conlow

A Fifty-Minute™ Series Book

This Fifty-Minute™ book is designed to be "read with a pencil." It is an excellent workbook for self-study as well as classroom learning. All material is copyright-protected and cannot be duplicated without permission from the publisher. *Therefore, be sure to order a copy for every training participant by contacting:*

Menlo Park, California

1-800-442-7477

CrispLearning.com

Excellence in Supervision
Essential Skills for the New Supervisor

Rick Conlow

CREDITS:
Senior Editor: **Debbie Woodbury**
Editor: **Eileen Cohen**
Production Editor: **Jill Zayszly**
Production Manager: **Judy Petry**
Design: **Nicole Phillips**
Cartoonist: **Ralph Mapson**

© 2001 Crisp Publications, Inc.
Printed in Canada by Webcom Limited

www.crisplearning.com

04   10 9 8 7 6 5 4

Library of Congress Catalog Card Number 2001087418
Conlow, Rick
Excellence in Supervision
ISBN 1-56052-611-4

Learning Objectives For:

EXCELLENCE IN SUPERVISION

The objectives for *Excellence in Supervision* are listed below. They have been developed to guide you, the reader, to the core issues covered in this book.

THE OBJECTIVES OF THIS BOOK ARE:

❑ 1) To describe the new roles and responsibilities that accompany a promotion to supervisor

❑ 2) To explain the principles and processes of performance management

❑ 3) To provide guidelines for communicating effectively with employees, peers, and managers

❑ 4) To explore how effective coaching skills can lead to increased employee satisfaction and productivity

❑ 5) To provide supervisors with strategies for dealing with organizational change

ASSESSING YOUR PROGRESS

In addition to the learning objectives, Crisp Learning has developed an **assessment** that covers the fundamental information presented in this book. A 25-item, multiple-choice and true-false questionnaire allows the reader to evaluate his or her comprehension of the subject matter. To learn how to obtain a copy of this assessment, please call **1-800-442-7477** and ask to speak with a Customer Service Representative.

Assessments should not be used in any employee selection process.

About the Author

Rick Conlow is president of Conlow Consulting Group and senior partner with Watsabaugh-Conlow Solutions. He brings bottom-line results to companies through leadership, quality improvement, customer service, team building, and sales programs. He has helped organizations reduce complaints by 57%, improve business by 20%, and win 33 quality service awards. Rick achieves results because of his hands-on, practical experience as a general manager, vice president, training director, national sales trainer, and consultant. Rick is also the author of *Excellence in Management, Returning to Learning,* and *Moments of Magic.*

You may contact Rick Conlow at raconlow@visi.com or (651) 482-8102.

How to Use this Book

This *Fifty-Minute™ Series Book* is a unique, user-friendly product. As you read through the material, you will quickly experience the interactive nature of the book. There are numerous exercises, real-world case studies, and examples that invite your opinion, as well as checklists, tips, and concise summaries that reinforce your understanding of the concepts presented.

A Crisp Learning *Fifty-Minute™ Book* can be used in variety of ways. Individual self-study is one of the most common. However, many organizations use *Fifty-Minute* books for pre-study before a classroom training session. Other organizations use the books as a part of a system-wide learning program—supported by video and other media based on the content in the books. Still others work with Crisp Learning to customize the material to meet their specific needs and reflect their culture. Regardless of how it is used, we hope you will join the more than 20 million satisfied learners worldwide who have completed a *Fifty-Minute Book.*

Preface

So you're about to become a supervisor for the first time, or have recently become one. You probably have mixed emotions. On one hand, you're excited about the opportunities. You'll be able to help and work with employees as no supervisor ever did with you! Yet, you also have concerns. Can you do it? How will your new peers accept you? What will the employees, some of them friends, think of you now? Where do you start?

Whatever your emotions, they're okay. It's not unusual to have some reservations while you look forward to the job. The good news is that *Excellence in Supervision: Essential Skills for the New Supervisor* will be a great help. Its purpose is two-fold: to help you start off on the right track today, and to provide you with practical and proven strategies for succeeding over time.

As a supervisor, you'll lead other people. As a leader, always remember that your employees' success is your success. You may still be required to do some of the tasks that the employees do; however, you'll also be responsible for getting things done through others. You won't be able to do it all alone.

This book is dedicated to helping you quickly learn and immediately apply the people skills of supervising. Most supervisors who fail do so because they have poor people-handling skills, not because they lack technical job skills. The five parts of the book outline and describe the critical success factors you need to create a positive, powerful, motivating environment for your employees. You will be challenged with application exercises to put the strategies discussed into practice. At the end of each section, you will review key strategies and include them in your action planning.

It's been said that winning isn't everything; the will to prepare to win is everything. Achieving excellence means knowing and doing those things that others are unwilling to learn or act on. Now, let's get started!

Positively,

Rick Conlow

Rick Conlow

Dedication

This book is dedicated to my wife Kelli and our children: Cian, Brendan, Siobhan, and Dania

Contents

Introduction

How many squares do you see?

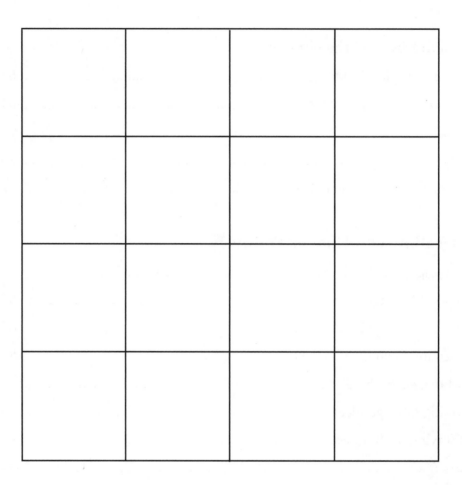

At first glance, most people see 16 or 17. By continuing to look at the image, you'll see the potential of 30 squares.

At first glance, you may recognize only a small percentage of your potential as a supervisor. With commitment, training, persistence, and a little help you'll be able to reach the potential of excellence in supervision! Now, let's make it happen!

P A R T 1

Getting Started

"*Leadership is the ability to decide what is to be done and then to get others to want to do it.*"

–Dwight D. Eisenhower

2

The Opportunity

You are in for an exciting journey. As a general rule, supervisors have more responsibility and make more money than other employees. Supervising also involves more work and greater stress. Supervisory positions are challenging because you become responsible for more results even though you don't do all the jobs. That's the opportunity. If you can improve performance through your efforts with a small group, you can do it with larger groups as you learn more, develop your skills, and progress in your career.

Why Do You Want to Supervise Others?

Place a check (✔) next to all the reasons that apply.

- ❏ To increase your job satisfaction

- ❏ To challenge your skills

- ❏ To learn and grow

- ❏ To gain more responsibility

- ❏ To make more money

- ❏ To achieve a personal goal

- ❏ To gain confidence

- ❏ Other:_____

Make no mistake about it, there will be problems. A new supervisor called a close friend after work one night and said, "Bill, I can't stand it. Every day, people are late or absent. And sometimes, the quality of the work is so poor. What's the matter with these employees? I don't know if I'm cut out for this."

Many people become supervisors because they have skill or experience in doing a particular job. Whatever your reason, doing the job while supervising others is a different ball game from just doing the job. Successful supervisors have a unique skill set that you'll learn in this book. These skills involve understanding the dynamics of working through people, communicating well with others, learning performance-management skills, effectively coaching others, and handling change positively.

How Do You Transition to Supervisor?

When you transition to supervisor, three key areas need your attention:

➤ Personal needs

➤ Other departments' needs

➤ Employees' needs

This book will give you ideas, applications, and strategies for all areas. First you must clarify your role, goals, and job description. That's what this chapter is about. Next, you need to smoothly begin working with others. In addition to serving external customers, treat other departments as customers also. Get to know your internal customers, listen to their concerns, and improve your area's service with them.

Often, the most critical transition is with the employees. Sometimes it is awkward, especially if some are your friends. Here are some tactics that will help you get off on the right foot. Place a check (✔) next to all that you feel you can do. Add any other thoughts.

First Steps

❏ Have your manager introduce you in your new role at a meeting.

❏ At the meeting, explain your excitement and other feelings about the job.

❏ Keep your early interactions with employees "low key." Don't come off too strong.

❏ Meet with employees one-on-one to discuss their jobs. Keep the first time informal. Listen and ask for ideas to make things better.

❏ Hold a department or work-group meeting. Be positive and discuss your goal to help reach the department's objectives. Share company information you may have.

❏ Observe people in action, help out where appropriate, and listen for ways to improve.

❏ Ask a few employees for their thoughts on changes you may want to make. Seek their input.

❏ Introduce changes more slowly if performance is good. Change things more quickly if performance is poor.

❏ Other:_____

The Definition of a Supervisor

A training consultant was conducting a seminar for new supervisors at a large manufacturing company. After a couple of sessions, one of the participants told the consultant that she liked the class but, more important, appreciated the references to working *with* or *through* employees. She commented that most supervisors she knows tell employees that they work *for* them. The participant added, "There is a difference."

A supervisor must work with and through employees to get the job done on time with the highest quality and within budget. *Excellence in Supervision means achieving positive results through people.* It's called influencing people. Influencing skills involve two types of power:

➤ **Personal Power:** influencing people to do things because they "*want to*"

➤ **Position Power:** influencing people to do things because they "*have to*"

Excellent supervisors positively influence people: employees, co-workers, and customers. They do it with extraordinary personal power. This book will give you skills and strategies to do this.

To start, answer the questions on the next page about experiences you've had that will help you become an excellent supervisor.

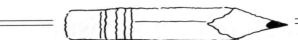

DEFINING EXCELLENCE

Learning from your past experiences will help you do well as a supervisor. Answer each question below to help you define excellence in supervision.

1. From your experience, what makes employees respect a supervisor?

_____

_____

2. From your experience, what causes employees to dislike a supervisor?

_____

_____

3. How do you want to be viewed as a supervisor? Is there anything you need to learn to help you achieve that?

_____

_____

4. What skills do you already have that will help you succeed?

_____

_____

5. What definition would you give to an excellent supervisor?

_____

_____

The Role of a Supervisor

What is your role as a supervisor? Place a check (✔) next to any roles that apply, or add your own:

❏ Produce a part or create product

❏ Perform a service

❏ Fix a technical problem

❏ Correct a mechanical failure

❏ Lead a creative team

❏ Sell a product or service

❏ Organize a marketing plan

❏ Serve the public

❏ Help serve patients

❏ Provide customer service

❏ Create a computer solution

❏ Educate students

❏ Administer public safety

❏ Solve problems

❏ Transport people

❏ Others:_____

What duties will you perform in order to fulfill your role? For example, if you provide customer service for a retail company, as a supervisor you will need to train employees, communicate with others, handle performance issues, build teamwork, and think creatively.

IDENTIFYING YOUR ROLE

Rank your top 10 of the following duties, from 1 to 10, for their importance in your role as a supervisor. Then, give yourself a (+) if you feel confident in that area and a (-) if you need to learn more.

1 = Most Important 10 = Least Important

Duties	Rank of Importance	Confidence Level (+ or -)
1. Handle problems fairly	_____	_____
2. Implement company policy	_____	_____
3. Delegate tasks	_____	_____
4. Train employees	_____	_____
5. Handle change positively	_____	_____
6. Recognize employees	_____	_____
7. Maintain a safe work area	_____	_____
8. Make decisions	_____	_____
9. Communicate effectively	_____	_____
10. Solves problem effectively	_____	_____
11. Think creatively	_____	_____
12. Complete reports on a timely basis	_____	_____
13. Gather employee suggestions	_____	_____
14. Build teamwork in employees	_____	_____
15. Take responsibility for results	_____	_____
16. Coach and motivate employees	_____	_____
17. Develop quality in the operation	_____	_____
18. Set standards and goals	_____	_____
19. Evaluate performance	_____	_____
20. Provide the proper equipment and tools	_____	_____

Note: These 20 items were the most common comments from supervisors who were asked to identify their roles.

The Responsibilities

Supervisors have tremendous responsibility in today's diverse workforce. Put a check (✔) next to the responsibilities below that you agree with and add others you believe are important.

❑ Recognize employees for a job well done.

❑ Treat all employees respectfully, fairly, honestly, and with dignity.

❑ Keep employees informed about the company and your area's goals and results.

❑ Be positive and encouraging to employees.

❑ Show interest in each employee as a person.

❑ Give employees an opportunity to learn and grow through ongoing training and education.

❑ Deal with performance issues consistently and fairly.

❑ Help employees develop teamwork and a sense of belonging.

❑ Be a good listener to employee problems and suggestions.

❑ Encourage initiative and new ideas.

❑ Communicate your belief in people's potential and the importance of the work being done.

❑ Support and represent your employees in the company.

❑ Accept your own mistakes openly and learn from them.

❑ Be accountable for your results. This is leadership.

❑ Other:_____

❑ _____

The Supervisor's Job Description

To succeed as a supervisor, you need to know your job description and how your success will be determined. Some companies provide written job descriptions. If your company does this, review it with your manager. If it doesn't, talk to your manager about your duties anyway. The ancient Chinese philosopher Lao Tzu said, "The journey of a thousand miles begins with the first step." You absolutely want to be stepping in the right direction. All good performance begins with:

➤ Clear expectations of the job duties and priorities

➤ Clear performance goals

In the pages that follow, you'll find a process for clarifying your expectations and goals.

A Sample Job Description

Read the sample job description below. Put a check (✔) next to the areas that pertain to your job. This is important for you and your employees because 80% of performance issues relate to unclear expectations, goals, and roles.

❏ Ensures that the department or work area achieves its goals in a quality and timely manner

❏ Trains and motivates employees to complete their job duties in a quality and timely manner

❏ Communicates regularly and effectively with employees and others at all levels

❏ Creates a positive work environment that supports good morale, quality work, and high productivity

❏ Implements and follows the human-resource and safety policies of the company or organization

❏ Develops teamwork within the work area or department and with other areas of the company

❏ Ensures that employees have the proper equipment and tools to do their jobs

❏ Completes all necessary paperwork and reports thoroughly and on time

❏ Maintains a work atmosphere that contributes to employees sharing ideas for continuous improvement

❏ Fulfills all related duties of the position

WRITING YOUR JOB DESCRIPTION

Write your job description in the space below. Then review it with your manager and discuss priorities.

_____

_____

_____

_____

_____

_____

_____

_____

_____

_____

_____

_____

_____

_____

_____

_____

_____

_____

_____

_____

_____

Management Thought: Old versus New

Management thought and practice has changed and improved since the early 1900s. The illustration below outlines the progression.

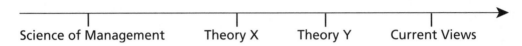

Science of Management   Theory X   Theory Y   Current Views

Influential management consultant Frederick Taylor preached the science of management in the early 20th century. Under his approach, people were like parts to a mass-production line. If everything was in its place, person and machine, the job could be controlled and produced efficiently.

The Theory X approach says employees don't like work and need to be closely controlled to perform. Theory Y's approach says employees do like work–get them involved and they'll succeed.

Recent studies suggest that the best managers and supervisors use both direction and participation to achieve excellent results. *Excellence in Supervision* supports this balanced, flexible approach.

More and more today, because of the rapid change in organizations, employees' performance can provide a company with a competitive advantage. Employee performance can make or break a company. Supervisors have the biggest influence on this. Supervisors need skills that help them get and keep the best people and then build employees into high-performing teams.

Two key questions are critical to a supervisor:

➤   What do employees need to succeed? (people issues)

➤   What does the organization need to achieve results? (production issues)

The chart on the next page differentiates old-school from currrent views.

MANAGEMENT STYLE

Put a check (✔) next to the words that describe how you want to be viewed.

OLD SCHOOL	NEW SCHOOL
❏ boss	❏ team leader
❏ authoritarian	❏ communicator
❏ controller	❏ coach
❏ organizer	❏ facilitator
❏ expert	❏ listener
❏ cop	❏ problem solver
❏ referee	❏ cheerleader

14

CASE STUDY 1

Read the quotes below about employees' experiences with poor supervisors. Then answer the questions.

"A few years ago, I had a supervisor that ruled with an iron fist. Life in the department was pretty miserable. It got to the point where I didn't want to go to work, let alone do anything while I was there. Each Monday, she would start riding/criticizing one person for the week. The following Monday, it was someone else's turn."

"The worst supervisor I had was narrow minded, had no vision, and always played it safe. He never tried anything new. So, he came off as a know-it-all. And, he would never stand up for you if the going got tough."

"One day I was working when my back and left side started to ache. I went to first aid, and they sent me to a clinic. The doctor said I had a pinched nerve. When I told my supervisor, the only thing he said to me was, 'I suppose you can't do anything now, can you?'"

"A supervisor I had never gave me any direction on a new project. I struggled to make progress. As time went on, I put in long hours to complete it and one week worked 20 hours on a Saturday. My supervisor even asked me to work Sunday with no recognition or support for all the other extra hours. I didn't, and he held it against me."

1. **What did the supervisors do that are examples of poorly working through others?** _____

_____

2. **How do you think these supervisors affected the performance of the employees?** _____

_____

3. **What can you learn or relearn from these four situations?** _____

_____

Compare your responses to the author's suggestions in the back of the book.

Strategies for Getting Started

Review the strategies below, put a check (✔) next to the ones you plan to use. For the strategies to work best, you need to adapt them to your situation using good judgment and common sense.

❑ **Obtain a copy of your job description.** Read it and then discuss it with your manager to clarify goals, expectations, and priorities. If no job description is available, use the one you made on page 11.

❑ **Talk to and interview three other supervisors or managers whom you admire.** Include only one from your company so you can obtain perceptions that are different from your current situation. Along with other concerns you have, ask them:

➤ How they help people stay motivated

➤ How they handle problems

➤ How they keep a good attitude

❑ **Make a plan to complete this book and act on the strategies.** Make a commitment to keep learning. Over the next six to 12 months, attend two seminars and read three other books. Include *Excellence in Management*, which is the next step after *Excellence in Supervision*. See the Recommended Reading list at the end of this book for other ideas.

❑ **Develop a written plan for your work area.** In the plan, outline goals related to your priorities and action steps to follow through. Review this with someone close to you to get some objective feedback. Then, meet with your manager to discuss it. Ask your manager for feedback, and make any needed adjustments.

❑ **Meet with your manager a couple of times a month for 30–60 minutes to review results.**

➤ Update him or her on your progress

➤ Discuss problems and your ideas for solutions

➤ Get input and new information from your manager

If your manager doesn't suggest these kinds of meetings, request them in a positive way. If he or she won't agree to the meetings, find another manager who is willing to help you with this. Creating, sharing, and refining your plan will help you focus, maintain a good attitude, and keep improving.

ACTION PLAN: GETTING STARTED

Create an action plan for your work area that will help you succeed in supervision. Add to the plan as you read this book and complete the activities. When you have completed the book, check your progress on the plan below and use the results to create a new action plan. *The Action Plan: Keep Excelling* in the back of this book will help ensure that you apply what you have learned and keep improving in your role as a supervisor.

1. Describe the goals and priorities for your department.

_____

_____

_____

_____

_____

_____

_____

_____

_____

_____

_____

2. List six action steps you will take to   Timeline
   prepare to win.

_____   _____

_____   _____

_____   _____

_____   _____

_____   _____

_____   _____

Managing for High Performance

"My experience with people is that they generally do what you expect them to do."

—Mary Kay Ash

Founder, Mary Kay Cosmetics

Performance Management

"How do I motivate people?" This is the question that supervisors and managers ask most commonly. The answer is the key to managing for high performance.

A mid-sized company was confronted with new competition. A number of its customers defected to competitors. Sales management set new standards for sales performance, conducted additional sales training, and created better incentives for success. The company's growth rate improved. Notice the strategies—goals, training, and recognition.

All people are motivated. It's just that some people aren't motivated to do what you want them to do. Practical experience and research give clues to key performance-management skills.

Key Skills for Managing Performance

➤ Set clear expectations and goals

➤ Give positive feedback

➤ Handle performance problems effectively

➤ Supervise with flexibility

Let's dig into the details of these practices so you can "get into action!"

THE BENEFITS OF MANAGING PERFORMANCE

Think of the supervisors you have worked with. Have they all set goals, given lots of feedback, handled problems positively, and supervised people with flexibility? Probably not.

Why don't more supervisors use these skills? Compare some of the benefits of using them to the obstacles that keep supervisors from exercising them. Add any additional benefits and obstacles you can think of.

Benefits

Why use these skills?

Builds confidence in employees

Clarifies goals and expectations

Generates pride in a job

Increases job satisfaction

Creates willingness to go the extra mile

Relieves job boredom or routine

Increases productivity

Other:

_____

_____

_____

Obstacles

Why aren't they used more?

Don't know how

Don't think the skills work

Don't want to change

Don't have enough time

Have tried and it didn't work

Laziness or apathy

Accept mediocre results

Other:

_____

_____

_____

Setting Expectations and Goals

All good performance begins with clear expectations and goals. Without these, employees seldom reach their potential. Unfortunately, nearly seven out of 10 supervisors and managers fail at it. Excellent supervisors do it well, and so can you.

A customer-service supervisor had poor customer-survey results in his department. After attending a seminar, he refocused his performance-management skills. With employee input, he set customer-satisfaction goals and a recognition plan for making progress and for accomplishing the goals. After six months, the department's customer-service ratings were better, and employee morale was extremely positive.

Supervisors must establish standards for performance. This way, employees will know what good performance looks like. Then you'll be able to evaluate more readily whether performance meets or exceeds expectations. Standards are most often written in terms of the goals to which they relate: quantity, quality, accuracy, timeliness, service, and relationships.

How to Establish Clear Expectations

Establish clear expectations by meeting with employees one-on-one. How frequently you do this will depend on the employee's experience level. Set up monthly or quarterly one-on-one meetings with experienced employees. Meet with inexperienced employees one-on-one during job training and in weekly or monthly sessions. The meetings should address the following issues:

➤ Explain the job during the hiring process. Make sure you are involved in the hiring of your employees or at least have some input. Go over the job description during the interview.

➤ During the initial meeting, create a job description or job-duties list for the employee. If the person is experienced, write the job-duties list together. If the person is inexperienced, you make the list. See the sample on page 24.

➤ Plan to review the job duties and goals regularly together. Focusing on priorities and goals, ask experienced employees for their input. Also ask them what they do well and what they can improve. Put the resulting decisions and agreements in writing so the two of you can review for progress later.

➤ With new employees, review the first day on the job and at the end of the first week. While this requires time, it will help the employee understand the job and succeed.

In addition to the one-on-one meetings:

➤ Focus on key job duties, goals, and results during monthly departmental or work-group meetings and in special training sessions you may conduct.

How to Set Goals

In each of the one-on-one meetings, you'll also discuss the performance goals or "standards" of the job. For most jobs, you determine three to five goals related to the priorities of the job. A goal needs to be SMART. This means:

S pecific

M easurable

A ttainable

R elevant

T ime-bound

Effective goal setting increases performance and productivity. Examples of goals are on page 25. (Just a note: some supervisors have 40 to 100 employees. This is unfortunate. The best range is seven to 10. It is nearly impossible to meet one-on-one with 20 or more people, so if you do supervise a large work group, team people up by job function. Identify team leaders to help you with the expectation-and-goals process.)

The biggest obstacle supervisors face in goal setting is finding adequate time to do it. Remember these two points:

➤ Lack of clear expectations and goals relates to 80% of performance problems

➤ Research shows that goal setting can improve performance 25% in areas where it hasn't been applied

Now, let's apply the material we've been talking about:

Step 1: Review the sample job description on the next page

Step 2: Review the sample goals on page 25

Step 3: Complete "Establishing Clear Expectations and Goals" on page 26

First, apply it to an employee you will work with. Then continue this process with all of your employees. Do this regularly, and people will perform better.

SAMPLE JOB DESCRIPTION

Customer Service Clerk

Overall Responsibility:

To ensure efficient department operations; provide prompt, friendly, courteous customer service; and maintain high-quality products for customers. This position reports to the Customer Service Supervisor.

Job Functions/Duties:

Customer Service

- Answer customer questions and complaints in a friendly, helpful, prompt manner or refer questions to the appropriate staff.
- Issue credits to customer for returned items as referred by cashiers, and ensure items are properly restocked, repaired, or disposed of.
- Help customer with placing and picking up special orders.
- Ensure a pleasant shopping environment.
- Provide price checks as requested by others.

Department Operations and Maintenance

- Clean up spills and messes promptly. Keep department working area in clean, orderly condition and retail area clear during shift.
- Accomplish what priority stocking needs to be done per shift.
- Process leftover deliveries as communicated by department manager.
- Communicate with supervisor and department manager any tasks needed to be done or opportunities to improve.
- Monitor all product for quality and dating. Pull products not meeting standards.
- Record damaged products accurately.
- Understand and utilize proper sanitizing procedures used during food preparation.

Personnel

- Help create a safe work environment.
- Maintain open, honest, and positive communications with all personnel.
- Use time efficiently while performing job functions. Set examples for other employees to observe.

Carry out appropriate opening and closing procedures as established by management.

Deal with equipment breakdowns during shift as needed.

Perform other job-related tasks assigned by management.

SAMPLE GOALS

1. Complete all action items on the project within **five** months and on budget

2. Produce a daily average of **580** units this month

3. Reduce cost by **10%** this quarter

4. Return all customer calls within **4** hours of receiving the message

5. Answer the phone within three rings **95%** of the time

6. Achieve on-time delivery **97%** of the time

7. Mail customer follow-up letters within **30** days after the sale

8. Achieve a customer-satisfaction index of **98%** or better each month

9. Sell **10** units each month for the next **three** months

10. Reorganize the service database by **August 15**

11. Complete the financial statement by the, **10th** day, of each month

12. Accomplish **90%** or better productivity each month

13. Increase sales by **10%** this year

ESTABLISHING CLEAR EXPECTATIONS AND GOALS

Name:_____

Job:_____

Overall Responsibility:

Key Job Duties:

Mark priorities with an asterisk (*), mark strengths with a plus sign (+), and mark areas to improve with a check mark (✔).

Performance Goals (SMART):

Complete a copy of this form for each of your employees.

Giving Positive Feedback

It's been said that "feedback is the breakfast of champions." Feedback can be positive or negative and, when used correctly and appropriately, both are acceptable means of managing employee performance. Clearly, it is more pleasant to give and receive positive feedback. When done correctly, constructive negative feedback can help employees better understand what is expected of them and how their actions contribute to success—for themselves and for the organization.

It all begins with positive recognition and praise. Over 90% of employees want more recognition. Have you ever received too much recognition? There are the basic principles to keep in mind.

Principles of Recognition

> Be specific   *"Thanks for staying late..."*

> Be as immediate as possible   *"Thanks for staying late tonight..."*

> Relate the recognition to the   *"Thanks for staying late tonight to*
>   activity/result   *complete that rush order..."*

> Relate the recognition to the person   *"Thanks for staying late*
>   *tonight to complete that*
>   *rush order, Bill..."*

> Be sincere and genuine   *"Thanks for staying late tonight to*
>   *complete that rush order, Bill. I*
>   *appreciate it."*

> Give weekly recognition.   *"Good job meeting the deadline on*
>   *that marketing plan this week."*

> Praise progress, not just   *"Your response times are*
>   accomplishment   *getting closer to your goal and I*
>   *appreciate how hard you are*
>   *working on that."*

Positive feedback can also take the form of rewards and recognition, but be sure any such gestures also follow the principles above. And never assume the gesture takes the place of specific, personalized praise—tell the employee why he or she is being rewarded and add your sincere thanks.

PROVIDING REWARDS AND RECOGNITION

Put a check (✔) next to the things you can do to provide no-cost and low-cost recognition, and add your own ideas. Then outline a plan of what you intend to do, keeping in mind the principles of recognition.

No Cost

❑ Say thank you

❑ Praise an employee in front of others

❑ Give recognition in a newsletter

❑ Give out thank-you notes

❑ Send a letter of praise to the family

❑ Post positive comment letters on a bulletin board

❑ Send verbal praise in a voicemail or email

❑ Compliment an employee for effort

❑ Give words of encouragement

❑ Send your manager a positive memo
about the employee and copy the employee

Low Cost

❑ Buy the employee lunch

❑ Give $10 cash

❑ Take people to a ball game

❑ Give a gift certificate

❑ Give out T-shirts or caps

❑ Award a trophy

❑ Award a certificate

❑ Distribute lapel pins

Your ideas and plans:

_____

_____

_____

_____

_____

Handling Performance Problems

You will, at times, have to give negative but constructive feedback. It's a key to high performance and motivation. If employees don't know what's wrong or don't realize their mistakes, how will they improve? For example, Olympic athletes get regular positive and negative feedback from their coaches during workouts.

As a general rule, there are no bad people, just some with behavior problems. An employee in a mechanical-contracting company had a hard time completing important customer reports on time. In other areas of the job, he did fine. Just telling him to complete the reports didn't change the behavior. Through regular review sessions, he improved.

Review sessions are one-on-one meetings for the purpose of giving constructive feedback to improve poor performance in an employee. A review session takes two general directions:

➢ **Counseling:** use a mutual discussion process for occasional problems

➢ **Disciplinary:** use a directive process for chronic or ongoing problems

When using either approach, keep the feedback simple and straightforward, and keep in mind the following principles.

Principles for Giving Constructive Feedback

➤ Be as immediate as possible

➤ Be specific about the problem

➤ Clarify your expectations, goals, and plans

➤ Avoid judgmental criticism

➤ Treat the person respectfully

Counseling Method

Most employees want to do a good job. Could you even imagine an employee saying, "I'm no good. I want to fail." Some employees just need extra help. It's human to make mistakes. In these cases, sit down with them, privately, using these steps.

1. **Identify the problem.**

   "I want to talk to you about being late to work. This is unacceptable because..."

2. **Ask for the employee's view.**

   "Please explain to me why this is happening."

3. **Seek the employee's ideas on how to improve. Add your guidance.**

   Ask: *"What can you do to improve?*

                     "What else can you do?"

   Add your ideas: *"What if you try..."*

4. **Agree on a plan and put it in writing.**

   "So, the plan we discussed is..."

5. **Establish a follow-up review of results.**

   "Let's discuss results next week. Same time and place."

This needs to be two-way communication. Conduct it in a positive way. Be constructive, not critical. Focus on the problem but do not threaten the employee's self-esteem. Avoid judgmental comments like, "It's stupid to do what you do," or "You're a poor employee because of this."

Disciplinary Method

A different, but essential part of the supervisior's job is to take disciplinary action when warranted. This may be warranted when an employee purposely violates company policy. Or when nothing you do—establishing goals, providing recognition, one-on-one communication, or even counseling—helps an employee to improve. It may come to the point where you need to fire the person.

To protect the employee's rights, yourself, and your company, there are specific steps you need to take leading up to this final action. Most companies have disciplinary procedures that include verbal and written warnings. Be sure you are familiar with and follow those procedures. Here are general steps to follow in most cases:

1. Identify the problem.

"Sara, the reason I want to talk with you is that your service contracts are below performance. We have talked about this before and created plans for improvement."(Include this statement if you actually have done this.)

2. State the expectation or goal.

"As you know, the goal of the department is..."

3. State the consequence.

"Because of the poor performance, I'm giving you this reprimand, which I'm also documenting in your file. Continued poor performance could lead to termination."

4. Ask for employee comments, then summarize.

"Sara, what we have discussed is.... I believe you can do this, and my hope is that you improve."

Handling Peformance Problems (CONTINUED)

Whenever you get to this stage, make certain that you:

➤ Clearly understand company policies regarding discipline and termination. If not, get help from the human resources department or your manager.

➤ Talk things over with human resources and your manager.

➤ Are consistent and clear in setting expectations and goals, giving feedback, providing training, and communicating with the employee.

Discipline issues are serious for both the employee and you. The employee's livelihood and self-esteem are at stake. The potential turnover can cause your company lost productivity, low morale, and wasted training dollars. Be sensitive, seek guidance, but also take action.

IDENTIFYING PERFORMANCE PROBLEMS

Which of the following performance problems do you anticipate you will need to address in the near future? Put a check (✔) next to any that relate to your current situation, and add any additional issues you are facing. Then make a plan to use either counseling or discipline to begin improving employee performance.

Potential Performance Problems

- ❑ Poor service or workmanship
- ❑ Absenteeism
- ❑ Missed deadlines
- ❑ Performance below expectations
- ❑ Tardiness
- ❑ Difficulty getting along with others
- ❑ Customer complaints about the person
- ❑ Critical or negative about work and the company
- ❑ Poor communication
- ❑ Lack of follow-through
- ❑ Other:

Counseling or Discipline?

Describe a situation where you need to or anticipate needing to use the counseling method. _____

_____

_____

Describe a situation where you need to or anticipate needing to use the disciplinary method. _____

_____

_____

Supervising with Flexibility

Supervising with flexibility means working with employees according to their needs and situation. Remember, all employees need goals, recognition, and help with performance problems. While you will try to apply your approach and company policies fairly, you will need to supervise individual people differently to help them perform at their best. For example, some employees need more training than others, some employees need more pats on the back or recognition, and a few require a lot more direction from you. Behavioral scientist Dr. Ken Blanchard calls it, "Different strokes for different folks." The first step involves analyzing an employee in two areas:

Motivation: This involves a person's willingness and desire to do the job. Does the employee "want to" and believe she can do the job?

Skill: This area takes into consideration experience at doing a job. Does the employee have the knowledge and ability to perform well?

As a supervisor, your job is to help enhance employees' willingness and ability to perform the job successfully. As already discussed, you can help employees increase their motivation and skills by setting expectations and goals, giving direction, and providing feedback. Another key to excellence in supervision is *flexibility*: determining how to best help each employee, according to the individual's current needs and situation. As you gain experience, you will develop a variety of tools and techniques that work for you. Initially, however, you can apply two basic approaches for managing for high performance: The Relationship Approach (RA) and the Training Approach (TA).

Relationship Approach

As you recall from Case Study 1, supervisors can negatively influence their employees' motivation to do the job. There is no good excuse for this. Certainly, there will be a time when nothing you do as a supervisor seems to change a negative attitude. You won't win them all. But an excellent supervisor positively improves the performance of a department or work group and is invaluable to the company. Excellent supervisors apply the right approaches that motivate and train their employees for greater success.

A new supervisor was once asked by the president of her company, "How do you motivate people?" She responded by saying, "All people motivate themselves for their own goals. However, I will create an atmosphere in my area where they decide to be excited and motivated to reach our department goals." The president smiled and welcomed the new supervisor to the company. The Relationship Approach means creating a positive and motivating work environment. When using this method, you focus more on the person's motivation than on his or her skill. You spend more time encouraging and supporting than training.

The best supervisors use goals, performance counseling, and recognition as key strategies with all employees. They also seek to better understand each individual. What is their "hot button?" In other words, what motivates them? For example, if it is fishing, ask them about it once in a while. Other actions to take include:

➤ Encourage the employee

➤ Ask for input and listen to the employee's ideas

➤ Solve problems with the employee

➤ Be positive and enthusiastic

➤ Check in with the person every day

➤ Give regular praise

Supervising with Flexibility (CONTINUED)

Understanding Employee Needs

In a survey, *Total Quality Newsletter* found people to be motivated by these top five issues:

1. Challenges (goals, risks, change, learning)

2. Recognition for a job well done

3. A feeling of being in on things (teamwork, input, opportunity)

4. Job security

5. Money

Unfortunately, most supervisors and managers think money is the most important motivator. As a supervisor, focus on the top three areas listed above and you will find you have a highly motivated, high-performing group of employees. You will find that even your most experienced employees can reach new levels of accomplishment when you help renew their enthusiasm by providing for these needs and building strong relationships and trust.

Training Approach

A supervisor is often required to do on-the-job training (OJT) for employees who are inexperienced in a particular job, task, or skill. With OJT, you invest more time in training and less on motivation.

OJT begins with clear expectations and goals, as we discussed earlier. Then, either the supervisor or a lead person needs to teach and guide the inexperienced employee on how to do a job or task. A lead person is a highly skilled employee with a willingness to help others learn on the job.

For OJT to be effective, it involves four basic phases, called P3+E.

Present

Describe, in detail, how to do the job. First, give an overview of the process. Then describe each step in the process, one at a time. It is helpful to have instructions that have been written as procedures. Finally, demonstrate how to perform the task as you explain the steps again.

Practice

Give the employee an opportunity to try doing the task, usually one step at a time. Encourage the person and correct any mistakes. Include enough practice until the person does it right a few times. Then move on to the next task or training phase.

Perform

Allow the employee a trial to perform solo. Do this for a reasonable period of time for the job.

Evaluate

After the trial period, review results. Point out the positives and correct any errors constructively. If the employee needs more training, start over with the Present phase. If not, extend the trial period or begin training on a new task or goal.

Supervising with Flexibility (CONTINUED)

Most supervisors go from Present to Perform, which isn't effective. If you use lead people, make sure you teach them how to use P3+E. In fact, use this approach to teach your leads how to train other employees.

Excellent supervisors also encourage employees to participate in company-sponsored training opportunities. If your company offers courses or sends employees to outside programs, encourage your employees to participate. Plan for their involvement in two to four sessions a year. While this could leave you temporarily shorthanded in the near term, in the long term your employees will perform better in their jobs and productivity and quality will improve.

Performance Assessment

Another aspect of supervising with flexibility is assessing the employee's performance level. Is the level below expectations (B), meet expectations (M), or exceed expectations (E)?

Performance Level

Performance can be assessed on an overall basis or on the basis of meeting specific criteria. For example, a salesperson in a financial company may be rated on overall company performance, based on sales revenue. To assess performance in specific areas, you would need to look at individual standards or goals. For example, a computer technician might be rated separately on these areas of performance:

Goal Area	Current Performance Level
Quality of Work	M (meets expectations)
Timeliness of Work	E (exceeds expectations)
Teamwork with Others	B (below expectations)

In this example, the computer technician is doing fine in the first two areas. In the third, it is determined that his lack of cooperation with peers is causing production delays. The supervisor is coaching him in this area.

APPLYING A FLEXIBLE APPROACH

Assess your employees using the chart below. Then make a plan to improve performance, as needed, using either the Relationship Approach (RA) or the Training Approach (TA). This is an immediate way to apply the strategy of supervising with flexibility.

Rate each employee's current level of motivation, skill, and results. Then determine a course of action for improvement.

M=Motivated **LM**=Lacks Motivation **S**=Skilled **US**=Unskilled

B=Below Expectations **M**=Meets Expectations **E**=Exceeds Expectations

Employee/Job:_____   **Date:**_____

Goal or other measurement area	Motivation M/LM	Skills S/US	Results B/M/E	Approach RA/TA

Comments: _____

_____

CASE STUDY 2

A new team leader position became available in a manufacturing plant. Three employees were recommended to the supervisor for the promotion— Joe Blue, John Evers, and Maria Sanchez. Joe has been with the company for 18 years and is highly skilled in the technical aspects of the operation. He is a loner and seldom talks to anyone. John has been with the company for 10 years, and his job results meet expectations. He gets along well with his co-workers and participates in many after-work activities with them. Maria has been with the company 12 years. Her productivity exceeds expectations, and she is rated among the best in the company. Most of her co-workers are male, and they often good-naturedly kid her for working so hard.

1. **Which employee do you think would transition to team leader most successfully?** _____

   _____

   _____

   Why? _____

   _____

   _____

2. **What are reasons you didn't choose the others?** _____

   _____

   _____

   _____

   _____

Compare your responses to the author's suggestions in the back of the book.

Strategies for Managing Performance

Review the strategies and put a check (✔) next to the ones that can work best for you. Add the selected strategies to your action plans.

- ❑ **Hold a meeting with your work group** (if you haven't already done so). Explain your excitement about the job, your desire to help, your expectations for positive results, and your goal to meet with each of them one-on-one. Answer any questions and share any company information that is new. This is particularly helpful if you supervise former co-workers or friends.

- ❑ **Meet with each employee one-on-one for 15 to 20 minutes.** During that time, focus positively on:

  - ➤ Getting to know the individual or just talking about the job

  - ➤ Asking for help or suggestions from the employee

  - ➤ Reviewing your overall expectations

  - ➤ Outlining the goal-setting process

  Note: If you have 10 or more employees, do the above in small groups or identify team leaders to meet one-on-one with employees. Take time to train the team leaders in effective one-on-one communication skills.

- ❑ **Be available to employees.** Every day, observe your employees in action. Talk to them informally. Help out with problems if necessary. Be constructive. Be a good listener. Praise progress and be encouraging. Notice areas that need improvement and begin identifying ideas where you can make positive changes.

- ❑ **Make an effort to work cooperatively with other work areas or departments.** Get to know the other supervisors. Be a good listener to learn how your area can do a better job. Be positive and try not to get caught up in negative feelings or complaining.

- ❑ **Make necessary changes.** If the department or work areas are performing poorly, make changes more quickly. Be sure to talk the changes over with your manager first. Also, thoroughly explain the *why* and *how* of all changes to your employees. If the work areas are performing well, make changes more slowly.

3

Communicating

with Others

Proactively

> *By definition, communication means two-way communication. Insecure indivduals don't like it. Bosses don't like it, but leaders and innnovators do like it.*"

—**Mark Shepard,** *Consultant*

44

Building Interdependent Relationships

In human relationships, there are two major options:

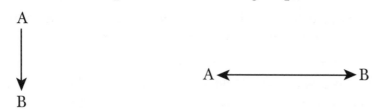

Dependent = Subordination   Interdependent = Equality

In a dependent relationship one person has most of the power and influence. Person A speaks and B does what he is told. In an interdependent relationship more equality exists. Even though person A may have the authority or position power, she shares it. In most relationships, which option is preferred?

An interdependent relationship is preferred because it builds trust, credibility, and rapport. To achieve excellence in supervision, you need interdependent relationships with employees. They promote the highest morale and productivity. Employees perform better because they want to.

Employees' perceptions of issues or problems often differ from their supervisor's perceptions. Unless the supervisor applies key communication skills, the different views can lead to conflicts. The conflicts can cause a lack of trust, rapport, and cooperation

To counteract this, many supervisors and managers resort to autocratic, dependent-relationship approaches to supervising. They act like a bull in a china shop. While short-term they may get where they are going, they leave a mess behind. The by-products are employee ill will and low morale.

Use the Key Communication Skills Checklist on the next page to help you communicate better. You will develop interdependent relationships with employees. They will have better morale, productivity, and attitudes.

46

KEY COMMUNICATION SKILLS CHECKLIST

Rate yourself on a scale of 1–5 by circling the most appropriate rating for each item. Add all circled numbers to determine your total score.

1=Rarely 2=Infrequently 3=Sometimes 4=Often 5=Most of the Time

When you finish, put a plus sign (+) next to three strengths and a check (✔) next to two areas that need improvement.

As a supervisor, I...

1. Take the time to communicate with others   1 2 3 4 5
2. Listen to others' ideas, especially when I disagree   1 2 3 4 5
3. Question the other person to gain more information   1 2 3 4 5
4. Paraphrase my understanding of the issue   1 2 3 4 5
5. Ask for input from others   1 2 3 4 5
6. Acknowledge others' feelings, even if they are negative   1 2 3 4 5
7. Treat others with respect and dignity   1 2 3 4 5
8. Seek solutions that can be mutually agreed to   1 2 3 4 5
9. Follow through on my commitments   1 2 3 4 5
10. Follow up to ensure positive communication   1 2 3 4 5
11. Pay attention to the person through good eye contact and helpful body language   1 2 3 4 5
12. Overall, demonstrate that I care about the other person's situation or need   1 2 3 4 5

Summary   TOTAL _____

60 – 55	Excellent, you are on your way to great communication. Keep learning!
54 – 44	Okay. You're doing a lot right. Stay focused and keep learning!
44 or below	This is an opportunity to improve. Make a commitment to keep learning!

Communicating One-on-One with Employees

A large shipping company was having productivity problems. Employees were concerned about a lack of communication. Management implemented a one-on-one policy. Formally, twice a year, all supervisors were required to meet with employees to review performance. Informally, they were to meet quarterly to discuss progress. Over time communication, morale, and productivity improved. Why was a policy necessary? Too many supervisors were reactive, not proactive, in their communication process.

Purpose of One-on-One Discussions

Earlier, we discussed the power of goals. The expectation and goal-setting process requires one-on-one meetings with employees. Here are other ways to use the one-on-one process. Put a check (✔) next to the ones you have used:

- ❏ Discuss performance issues

- ❏ Give recognition

- ❏ Listen to personal problems

- ❏ Conduct a coaching session

- ❏ Solve problems

- ❏ Brainstorm new ideas

- ❏ Delegate a task

Too often, supervisors won't take the time for one-on-one meetings because they are too busy. *A supervisor who is too busy for employees is too busy to be a supervisor.* Daily informal one-on-ones can happen in a couple of minutes. Formal one-on-ones need to be done weekly to quarterly depending on the job. You should meet with inexperienced people more often. You should also meet more often if there is a sense of urgency for better results. These meetings usually take 30 to 60 minutes and will be described in more detail in Part 4: Coaching for Excellence.

Benefits of One-on-One Communication

What's in it for you? Here are some of the benefits of conducting one-on-one meetings:

➤ Improve communication

➤ Eliminate some problems

➤ Prevent other problems

➤ Demonstrate respect and concern

➤ Increase morale

➤ Enhance performance and productivity

➤ Build rapport and trust

Delegating Tasks

Excellent supervisors delegate. Bill Marriott Sr., chairman and CEO of Marriott International, said, "Don't do anything someone else can do for you." The goals of delegating are:

➤ Give an employee a task she can do or can learn to do so you can accomplish other, more pressing goals

➤ Develop your employees' skills

➤ Accomplish better and faster results

Common Reasons for Not Delegating

Unfortunately, many leaders fail to delegate for a variety of reasons. Put a check (✔) next to any that apply to you:

❏ Lack of confidence in employees

❏ Lack of time to communicate about a task or train the employee in the task

❏ Personal pride and reward in doing a task

❏ Personal competence in a task and desire for it to be done right

❏ Fear of letting go of a task

❏ Don't know how to delegate

How to Delegate

Meet with the employee one-on-one and follow these steps:

1. Outline clear expectations, goals, and reasons for delegating the task.

2. Set timelines.

3. Answer any questions or concerns.

4. Reassure the employee that he can do it. Give needed tools, support, or training.

5. Follow up to check on progress.

A new sales manager was having trouble keeping up with his past accounts and finding new ways to grow the business. He analyzed his job priorities and decided to delegate some of his sales accounts to his salespeople. He soon found time to develop a needed advertising campaign.

Remember, a supervisor's success depends on employees' success. As a general rule, delegate to more experienced employees. Learn to delegate tasks that matter to the organization but are hard for you to do because of other priorities.

Use the chart on the next page to organize your thinking and prepare to delegate some tasks.

Make a Plan to Delegate

Task/Goal	Keep	Delegate	Why Delegate or Keep (remember the three goals)

Communicating with a Team

Together

Everyone

Achieves

More

Any time you supervise more than one person, teamwork issues arise. All the supervisory practices we have discussed will help build better teamwork. In Part 5: Dealing with Change Positively, other techniques are added. Another great tool for improving teamwork is to hold regular meetings. Usually monthly meetings will do. Consider the examples below:

Union employees complained about the lack of communication from the company. The supervisor expressed frustration, saying, "You can't talk to those people about company problems—they only care about their contracts."

At the urging of management, and with assistance from a consultant, the supervisor co-facilitated some meetings with the represented employees. The employees were updated on company news; their concerns were listened to, and they were asked for their input. Relationships strengthened, morale increased, and the situation improved. The supervisor changed from a dependent to an interdependent approach.

A customer-service department had poor customer survey ratings. To improve, the supervisor created a team of six customer service reps to represent the department. Over a period of months, the team met every week to identify the issues, gain input, and create a plan. After implementing the plan to improve responsiveness and courtesy, the customer-service rating improved.

A new supervisor for a financial-services company felt it was important to improve communication in her department. Performance was mediocre, and the previous supervisor had been fired. The new supervisor instituted weekly department meetings to share information and work on problems. Within a few weeks, performance and morale increased.

Use a Team Approach

Hold regular department or work-group meetings to:

➤ Share company and department information

➤ Discuss problems

➤ Recognize results

➤ Conduct training

➤ Communicate about performance results

➤ Create plans

➤ Brainstorm ways to improve

➤ Gain input

➤ Review changes

➤ Check on how people are doing

Guidelines for Team Meetings

Generally, regular weekly or monthly meetings last 30 to 60 minutes.
In all meetings:

➤ Have an agenda that you've prepared in advance

➤ Take notes or ask someone else to

➤ Start on time

➤ End on time

➤ Get others involved by asking for input and letting others present
material

➤ Be a good listener

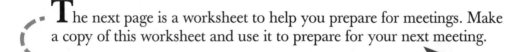

The next page is a worksheet to help you prepare for meetings. Make
a copy of this worksheet and use it to prepare for your next meeting.

MEETING PLANNER

Department_____   Date_____

Start Time_____   End Time_____

Agenda: Key Topics

Notes:

Communicating Every Day with Others

Jim was a superb supervisor and an excellent manager. When asked what his secret was, he replied with a smile, "Well, I didn't go to college." Then he laughed heartily! He added, however, his success had to do with his ability to communicate. He started every day by greeting or talking to employees in his area and, if time allowed, in other departments. The discussion focused on the employee's vacation, interests, family, or general news. Jim said, "We only talked business if they brought it up." Over time, rapport developed.

Management guru Tom Peters coined the term "MBWA–Managing By Wandering Around." It means to be available and to roll up your sleeves to interact and work with employees.

Evidence of Poor Communication

Some common complaints employees have about supervisors' poor communication skills include the following. Place a check (✔) next to the ones you have experienced as an employee, and add another from your experience:

- ❑ The supervisor is never around to talk things over or make a decision

- ❑ The supervisor is always in a meeting

- ❑ The supervisor spends too much time on the computer pounding out memos or reports

- ❑ The supervisor is unapproachable because of a negative attitude

- ❑ The supervisor claims to be too busy to listen about problems and concerns

- ❑ The supervisor never holds a department meeting

- ❑ Other:_____

Communication requires interaction with others. It is an investment. If you give your employees more of your time, they will give you more of their time. In other words, treat people with respect, talk to them, listen, and work with them. If you do this, others will give you their best and go the extra mile. Daniel Goleman, author of the book *Emotional Intelligence,* supports this. He found in his research that the best leaders have the best people skills. Isn't that what we've been discussing?

Communicating with Your Manager

A CEO was asked what was the number one characteristic that he looked for in a supervisor. He responded by saying, "Initiative!" In other words, a supervisor needs to take action and make things happen. This also applies to communicating with your manager. Some managers do a great job; others do a poor job. Regardless, you need to communicate upward.

Reasons for Communicating Upward

➤ Keep your manager informed of your progress

➤ Build your manager's confidence in your ability to get things done

➤ Minimize the problems your manager has to solve

➤ Get help when needed

➤ Share your ideas and solutions

A new supervisor quickly discovered he had personnel problems. Three out of seven employees were performing poorly. He wasn't sure what to do. His manager was the hands-off type and wasn't helpful. The supervisor talked to another manager to gain ideas on handling the performance issues. Then he created a plan for improvement for each individual. After updating his manager on the problems and solutions, the manager said, "Sounds good; do it!"

COMMUNICATING POSITIVELY WITH YOUR MANAGER

Check (✔) the items below that you will focus on:

❑ Stay on top of things and be aware of what is going on in your area and around the company.

❑ Be proactive, not reactive—seek ways to continuously improve.

❑ Be prepared with solutions to problems, rather than just bringing up problems.

❑ Write goals and plans and talk to your manager about them even it isn't requested.

❑ Meet with your manager weekly or monthly to discuss your progress.

❑ Keep your manager informed about problems or changes—no surprises!

❑ Follow through on commitments and timelines. Stay organized to track these.

❑ Go out of your way to build positive bridges with other departments. Treat them as internal customers.

❑ Clarify priorities; focus on what's most important.

❑ Take responsibility; don't blame others. If there are obstacles outside your control, identify ways to minimize them.

CASE STUDY 3

Cindy, a recently promoted supervisor, wants to delegate ordering of office supplies and equipment to Jim. Cindy is extremely busy with other priorities. The following discussion took place:

Cindy: *"Jim, I want you to begin ordering new supplies and to create a system to do it more effectively."*

Jim: *"I'm really busy. Besides, it's pretty routine, isn't it? Couldn't someone else do it?"*

Cindy: *"Everyone's busy. I've been doing it since I started, and it's time someone else took over. I don't have time anymore. Here are the old procedures. Let me know if you have questions or problems."*

Jim: *"But I do have some questions..."*

Cindy: *"See you later, Jim. I have a meeting."*

What are your reactions to how this delegation happened?

_____

_____

_____

What should Cindy do to follow up?

_____

_____

_____

What should Cindy do better or differently next time?

_____

_____

_____

Compare your responses to the author's suggestions in the back of the book.

Strategies for Proactive Communication

Review the strategies below, put a check (✔) next to the ones you will try. Add these to your action plans.

❑ **Make a commitment.** The Japanese use the term Kaizen, meaning continuous improvement. Use this focus for how you communicate. It's been said it's not your aptitude but your attitude that determines your altitude. Be willing to make communication improvement a lifelong process.

❑ **Prepare, prepare, prepare.** Use the Meeting Planner worksheet to prepare for all your meetings. If you take the time to think things through, you will come across as more positive and more professional.

❑ **Ask for feedback.** Ask your manager or someone you trust to give you feedback on how well you communicate. Ask this person to rate you on the Key Communication Skills Checklist. Listen to the feedback nondefensively.

❑ **Delegate tasks effectively.** A way to develop employees is to delegate. It also helps you manage your time better. Delegate priorities to more experienced people and routine tasks to inexperienced people. Effective delegation requires a clear definition of the goal, tasks, and timeline. Give training if needed. Don't ask someone to do a task and then look over his shoulder while he is doing it. This approach does not save you any time, and the employee will resent it.

When an employee succeeds at the delegated task, give timely and specific positive feedback. If the employee does not complete the task successfully, take time to review the steps the employee took, assess the results, and discuss ideas for succeeding next time. Then give the employee another chance. Remember, one of the objectives of supervision is to accomplish more through the work of others. It is your job to coach and counsel employees toward success.

❑ **Read other books.** See the Recommended Reading list in the back of this book for suggestions.

Coaching for

Excellence

> " *A Coach must keep everyone on the team in touch with present-moment realities—knowing where they stand, knowing where they're falling short of their potential, and knowing it openly and fairly.* "

–Pat Riley, *The Winner Within*

The Changing Playing Field

The playing field is changing in our business world. Changes are driven by four key forces outlined below.

Emergence of the Information Age

➤ Emerging technology creates higher expectations for productivity and responsiveness

➤ Ready availability and transmission of data creates information overload

Greater Competition

➤ Business improvements and innovations

➤ Multinational consolidation

➤ Entrepreneurial spirit

Increasing Customer Demands

➤ More choices for consumers

➤ Customers want it all: price, quality, service

➤ Word of mouth is faster via Internet

Volatile Workforces

➤ Less employee loyalty

➤ Diverse workforces

➤ Varied generational needs

➤ Labor shortages

Because of these, supervisors are under great pressure to do more with less. They are expected to be a liaison between employees and management, to increase productivity, to increase quality or service, and to build employee morale. To do this, many turn to the example set by those who serve the role of a coach—coaches of winning sports teams, voice coaches, and mentors in all areas of personal and professional development.

While the challenges are great, supervisors who can adapt and learn to coach for better results become extremely valuable to their companies. Coaching is an essential skill for all supervisors, and those who master it have learned key behaviors and characteristics that produce positive results.

The Best and Worst Supervisors

Think of the absolutely worst supervisor you ever worked with or knew about. What did the person do and what was the person's character? Then, think of the best supervisor you worked for or knew about. How was this person different? In both cases, describe the coaching behaviors and character of the person. Then compare the behaviors you listed with those on the next page.

Worst Behavior

1. _____
2. _____
3. _____
4. _____
5. _____

Character

1. _____
2. _____
3. _____
4. _____
5. _____

Best Behavior

1. _____
2. _____
3. _____
4. _____
5. _____

Character

1. _____
2. _____
3. _____
4. _____
5. _____

Coaching Behaviors of Supervisors

Research in work settings have established that these are the coaching behaviors of the least effective and most effective supervisors:

Worst Coaches	**Best Coaches**
➤ Set unclear expectations	➤ Establish clear expectations
➤ Set vague goals/standards	➤ Set clear goals/standards
➤ Give limited or vague feedback	➤ Give regular feedback
➤ Observe performance irregularly	➤ Observe performance regularly
➤ Provide only negative feedback	➤ Give constructive feedback
➤ Give limited positive recognition	➤ Recognize and reward accomplishments
➤ Offer little training	➤ Provide regular training
➤ Give sporadic advice	➤ Give helpful advice
➤ Spend more time on technical or administrative matters	➤ Invest the time to help
➤ Listen ineffectively	➤ Listen effectively
➤ Have poor people skills	➤ Have good people skills

Leadership Character

Kouzes and Posner are researchers and consultants who conducted an intense study of leadership in the 1980s and 1990s. Their study identified behavior and characteristics of the most successful leaders. Their results were published in the book *The Leadership Challenge*.

As a supervisor, you will be a leader of people. Notice the coaching characteristics you identified in the Worst/Best exercise. Consider how they relate to the top five traits created by Kouzes and Posner as described below.

1. Honesty

This involves ethics and integrity; people whose word is steadfast

2. Forward Looking

This involves longer-term thinking, not just short-term thinking

3. Inspiring

This means the ability to motivate or "fire people up"

4. Competent

Leaders are students of the game and are knowledgeable or willing to learn

5. Fair-Minded

This involves treating people consistently and, again, doing what's right

Who you are speaks louder than what you say. If you want people to put in extra time, *you* have to. If you need more teamwork, *you* be a team player. If communication problems exist, be a good listener. If more training is needed, *you* attend also. If respect is an issue, give others respect. If a decision needs to be made, make it.

On the next page is a coaching inventory. Rate yourself to discover your potential!

COACHING FOR EXCELLENCE INVENTORY

The behaviors of the best coaches translate into the practices below. Using the scale shown, rate yourself in these areas in terms of how often you engage in the following behaviors.

1=Never 2=Rarely 3=Sometimes 4=Often 5=Always

Be honest with yourself and answer as you think you really are, not what you should be.

_____ 1. I discuss agreed-upon goals and expectations with my employees.

_____ 2. I set aside uninterrupted and private time to meet with my employees.

_____ 3. I review my employee's goals and expectations at the start of each of my coaching sessions.

_____ 4. I encourage open discussion when I hold coaching meetings.

_____ 5. I ask my employees for their input when reviewing their performance.

_____ 6. I listen to and paraphrase what my employees are trying to say.

_____ 7. I carefully assess all factors that affect my employees' performance results.

_____ 8. I regularly observe my employees in action with customers or others.

_____ 9. I recognize and reward high performance.

_____ 10. I give regular and immediate feedback to my employees in a constructive manner.

_____ 11. I listen to my employees' feedback and concerns before giving my own.

_____ 12. I am specific about behaviors and tasks when I give advice or guidance.

_____ 13. I provide feedback that is appropriate to my employees' situations, performance level, and goals.

CONTINUED

======= CONTINUED =======

_____ 14. I teach my employees new skills clearly and systematically.

_____ 15. I develop specific action plans to help improve my employees' skills and results.

_____ 16. I gradually give more responsibility to my employees so they can grow.

_____ 17. I ensure that my employees understand and agree to their action plans.

_____ 18. I negotiate project tasks and deadlines with my experienced employees.

_____ 19. I set follow-up meetings at the conclusion of my coaching meetings.

_____ 20. I make sure that my follow-up coaching meetings take place.

COACHING FOR EXCELLENCE INVENTORY: SCORING

Write in your score for each number in the space below. Put a plus sign (+) by the top five numbers and a check (✔) by the lowest two. Then answer the questions.

Step 1: Review goals and expectations.

1. ____
2. ____
3. ____

Total ____

Step 2: Assess level of performance.

4. ____
5. ____
6. ____
7. ____
8. ____

Total ____

Step 3: Provide feedback/ guidance.

9. ____
10. ____
11. ____
12. ____
13. ____
14. ____

Total ____

Step 4: Develop action plans.

15. ____
16. ____
17. ____
18. ____

Total ____

Step 5: Establish follow-up.

19. ____
20. ____

Total ____

How can you make sure you take the time to coach? _____

_____

_____

What are your strengths? (list 3—5) _____

_____

_____

_____

How can you coach even more effectively? (list 2—3 ways) _____

_____

_____

The Coaching Process

There are two major types of coaching: formal and informal. By embracing the coaching concept, supervisors get more done in less time by helping the employees succeed. Coaching is the art of high performance. If you practice informal and formal coaching, employees may not like some of your decisions, but they will still respect you and get the job done.

Informal Coaching

Informal coaching involves the day-to-day relationship between the supervisor and the employee. First of all, is the relationship built on trust? All employees have what is called an emotional bank account. Author Steven Covey describes this in *Seven Habits of Highly Effective People*. It is either positive or negative. If it is positive, trust is present, and results and performance are good. If it is negative, trust is absent, and performance often suffers.

Just as with a real savings account, an emotional bank account requires deposits before you make withdrawals. So what do you do to make the emotional bank account positive and increase trust? Think about what *you* would want from a supervisor.

Think about all the principles and practices we have discussed so far. Many of these points under informal coaching are examples of the techniques and strategies you have been working on throughout *Excellence in Supervision*. If these kinds of actions are everyday practices, you'll create a surplus in the emotional bank accounts of employees. This is crucial because, at times, you'll have to make the tougher decision: change work hours, require overtime, discipline an employee, follow through on an unpopular decision by management, or act in opposition to an employee's idea of what is best. These are withdrawals, often viewed negatively. With a surplus of positives in the emotional bank account, employees will stay motivated.

POSITIVE PRACTICES

Put a check (✔) next to the items below that make sense to you. Notice all these actions can be done in a few minutes of time every day or over time.

- ❏ Greet the employee daily
- ❏ Talk about nonbusiness matters of interest to the employee
- ❏ Have lunch with employees
- ❏ Demonstrate courtesy and respect
- ❏ Learn and use people's names
- ❏ Be a good listener
- ❏ Have a sense of humor
- ❏ Deal with performance issues
- ❏ Do what you say you will do
- ❏ Treat people fairly
- ❏ Be considerate and understanding when dealing with personal matters
- ❏ Be positive
- ❏ Work side-by-side with employees on an important project
- ❏ Encourage others
- ❏ Give recognition for progress and results
- ❏ Help out when necessary
- ❏ Have some fun at work
- ❏ Buy someone a soft drink or coffee
- ❏ Other:_____

Formal Coaching

From the scoring sheet for the Coaching for Excellence Inventory (page 69), you'll notice there are five steps to the coaching process. This is for formal coaching. Formal coaching means talking one-on-one with employees to help them improve performance. Coaching involves a mutual problem-solving effort and it usually takes 30 to 60 minutes. Spending a few minutes on a problem isn't formal coaching, it's more likely just *telling* the employee what to do!

Another goal of formal coaching is developing employees' skills at thinking through problems and identifying solutions on their own. As a result, in the future employees will come to you with solutions to problems, not just the problems.

Under what circumstances do you do formal coaching? First, do it to help poor or marginal performers do better. Second, do it to help a good performer excel or handle a delegated project. And third, use it in times of change. Remember, you have to schedule coaching sessions or you will never seem to find time for them.

An office supervisor had an employee who generally met expectations except for the accounts-receivable goal. She usually missed timelines. After learning how to coach, the supervisor met with this employee weekly for 30 minutes. Following the coaching steps, the supervisor helped the employee meet the goal. The employee had some ideas for the action plan that helped integrate all her work. Afterward, monthly one-on-one goal meetings kept the employee on track.

The Formal Coaching Process

Here are more details of the formal coaching process.

Preparation:

1. Set clear goals and expectations. (Identify the employee's skill, motivation, and performance level.)

2. Do your homework and review the employee's current performance.

3. Provide regular performance feedback. Use informal coaching strategies regularly.

4. Set aside the time for a coaching meeting (30–60 minutes). Create a positive, friendly atmosphere.

The Coaching Process:

1. Review the goal/expectation. (Start the coaching session by clarifying the goal. Ask the employee to describe it.)

2. Assess the current level of performance from employee input. Ask the four key questions below. You will ask other questions, but these are the core questions:

   ➤ Overall, how are you doing?

   ➤ What's working?

   ➤ What isn't working?

   ➤ What can you do better or differently?

   Compare the employee responses to your observations and knowledge of their results.

3. Provide feedback and guidance. Comment on what the employee says.

4. Develop action plans with employee input. Give your ideas for the plan. Put the ideas for improvement in writing, add your recommendations, and gain agreement.

5. Establish follow-up steps. Summarize the discussion and set a specific date and time for the next meeting.

COACHING WORKSHEET: SAMPLE

Name: Bill Jones   **Date:** 2/15

1. **Performance Goals:** What is the key goal we are working on?

   - Improving the customer satisfaction rating to 95% or higher.

2. **Assess performance:**

   Employee Input: Supervisor, ask four key questions—take notes on comments
   - Overall, how are you doing?
   - What's working well?
   - What isn't working?
   - What will you do better or differently?

   Observations/results: Supervisor, note your observations of performance and any available data, such as customer survey results
   - Experiencing fewer complaints
   - Rating of 93.5 (last quarter)
   - Evidence that employee is following through on action plan

3. **Provide feedback/guidance:**
   - How about follow-up calls after customer contact?
   - No thank-you notes

4. **Develop action plans:**

   Employee's ideas:

       1. Act more courteously—say please, thank you, etc.

       2. Greet promptly—in less than one minute

   Supervisor's ideas:

       3. Do follow-up calls—within two days

       4. Send thank-you notes—daily

5. **Establish follow-up steps**

   Next meeting 2/28 at 3:00 p.m.

COACHING WORKSHEET

Using the preceding sample for guidance, fill this out for an employee situation you are currently involved in. For the purpose of this exercise, complete as much of the worksheet as possible, whether you have talked to the employee yet or not. As you begin implementing this technique with all employees, use this format as an outline for notetaking. Always give a copy of your notes to the employee.

Name:_____Date:_____

1. Performance Goals:

2. Assess performance:

   Employee input:

   Observations/results:

3. Provide feedback/guidance:

4. Develop action plans:

5. Establish follow-up steps:

CASE STUDY 4

1. Doug is a new employee in the advertising department. On his first day on the job, his supervisor, Kelli, met him for breakfast. After breakfast, they returned to the office and Kelli showed him around and made introductions. Kelli then met with Doug to review the day's agenda, his job duties, expectations, and goals. Doug had some questions, which they discussed. Afterwards, Kelli took Doug to personnel to handle necessary paperwork.

How do you think Doug felt about his first day? _____

_____

What has been your experience in this type of situation? _____

_____

How do you plan to handle an employee's first day? _____

_____

2. Ross is an experienced employee and a good performer. He's a financial consultant for a bank and is a loyal employee. However, he can do better. His new supervisor, Pat, has been meeting with all his employees one-on-one. In Pat's meeting with Ross, Pat explained his plan to do coaching. Ross reacted negatively and said, "I'm doing the best I can." In the first coaching session, Ross wasn't very talkative.

Why do you think Ross reacted this way? _____

_____

How do you engage someone who isn't very talkative in a meeting?

_____

What should Pat do? _____

Compare your responses to the author's suggestions in the back of the book.

Strategies for Effective Coaching

Review the strategies below. Put a check (✔) next to the ones you will attempt and add them to your action plans.

❑ **Discuss the results of the Coaching for Excellence Inventory with your manager or another supervisor.**

During the review, talk about strengths and areas to improve. Brainstorm ideas. Discuss different ways to help employees. Resist the temptation to think that "this doesn't apply to our situation." Coaching works! Excellent supervisors everywhere use coaching techniques.

❑ **Review how you have applied informal coaching.**

At the end of a work week, analyze what happened. What results did you achieve? Which employees had problems? Why? What worked? What didn't work? What can you learn or relearn? What will you do better or differently next week?

❑ **Complete a formal coaching session with an employee and document the results using the Coaching Worksheet in this book.**

What did you learn? If you're comfortable, discuss the process with your manager or another supervisor. Remember, set high standards for yourself and continue practicing these skills and improving your own performance as a coach.

❑ **Reward yourself!**

Becoming an excellent supervisor is not easy. Achieving excellence is difficult. Others, including your manager, may tell you not to waste your time coaching. There are obstacles. With persistence and determination, you'll experience the benefits—pride and self-satisfaction, as well as improved production and employee morale. So reward yourself! Go out to dinner, buy yourself something, relax!

Dealing with Change Positively

" *To improve is to change, so to be perfect is to have changed often.* "

—**Winston Churchill**

A New Paradigm

The human being is really a change artist. Scientists say that every cell in a human body is replaced every five to seven years. Literally, a person is a different individual numerous times in life. If we tried to eliminate this process of change we would die.

Following are a few experiments that illustrate how most people handle change. Try these for yourself:

➤ Clasp your hands together. Notice which thumb is on top. Now clasp your hands with the other thumb on top. How does it feel?

➤ Fold your arms in front of your chest. Notice which arm is tucked in. Now fold the arms with the other arm tucked in. How does it feel?

➤ Write your name somewhere on this page, as if you were signing a check. Now write your name again with your other hand. How does it look?

Most people handle change by resisting it. Did you try the three experiments? In the first two situations the change probably felt uncomfortable or weird. In the third situation, it was probably hard to write your name with the opposite hand. These are not unusual results. However, in the last scenario, if you no longer had your first hand, could you learn to write your name better with the other one? You could! Why? Because you would have no choice. You would have to learn.

In Part 4 we discussed the changing playing field. We outlined four forces that are driving change in our business environments. These forces are designing a new paradigm for the business world. They are creating a fast-paced interdependent dynamic marketplace. Organizations and people have to change to keep up. Change is the name of the game.

The four forces:

➤ Emergence of the information age

➤ Greater competition

➤ Increasing customer demands

➤ Volatile workforces

Charles Darwin said, "It is not the strongest of the species that survive, nor the most intelligent, but the one most responsive to change." How responsive or resistant are you to change? Do you see change as a problem or a possibility? There are two basic ways to change:

➤ **Proactive:** make a deliberate choice and plan to change

➤ **Reactive**: be forced to change

We can't control everything that happens to us, so at times we will need to react to changes. However, we can always control how we respond to changes and determine proactive steps to accelerate the positive effect of the changes we will experience.

Begin the process to deal with change more positively by completing the exercise on the next page.

THE REALITIES OF CHANGE

Think of a situation you have experienced or observed that featured the realities of our changing world and respond to these questions.

1. What was the situation? _____

_____

_____

_____

2. What changed? Why? _____

_____

_____

_____

3. How did people react? Why? _____

_____

_____

_____

4. What were the solutions? _____

_____

_____

_____

5. How did things work out? Then? Today? _____

_____

_____

_____

6. What can you learn or relearn from this experience? _____

_____

_____

Organizational Change

Our rapidly changing world creates tremendous pressure for companies to improve. Economist Joseph A. Schumpeler called the process of change in the economy "creative destruction." Old jobs fade away to new ones. Old companies change or give way to new ones. Nearly half of all the Fortune 500 companies of the 1980s are gone today. In order to survive, organizations have to adapt. Companies have used a variety of approaches to change organizationally. Put a check (✔) next to any of the following initiatives and changes you have experienced:

- ❏ Participative management
- ❏ Action teams
- ❏ Self-directed teams
- ❏ Total Quality Management
- ❏ Re-engineering
- ❏ Creating a vision
- ❏ The Learning Company
- ❏ Restructuring
- ❏ Decentralization/centralization
- ❏ Employee involvement
- ❏ Downsizing
- ❏ New technology
- ❏ Mergers/acquisitions
- ❏ Company policy/benefit revisions
- ❏ Reorganization
- ❏ New product introductions
- ❏ Relocation of offices/plants
- ❏ New leadership
- ❏ Strategic alliances
- ❏ New performance standards
- ❏ Layoffs
- ❏ Other _____

The Impact of Change

During change processes, employees usually experience one or more of these effects:

➤ Lower morale

➤ Higher stress levels

➤ More conflicts/problems

➤ Decrease in productivity

➤ Decrease service or quality

➤ Poorer attitudes

As a supervisor, your challenge is to counteract these negative reactions. Your job is to lead employees through their resistance to higher performance levels. The rest of this chapter will explore four tools or techniques for handling change more positively:

Four Techniques:

➤ Communicating change effectively

➤ Change-management skills

➤ Brainstorming

➤ Problem solving

In order to use these tools well, you may need to change your perceptions of employee potential and your approach to getting things done.

Communicating Change Effectively

A supervisory group had to deliver some good and bad news to a large manufacturing company. The good news: business was growing and orders increasing. The bad news: production needed to increase to meet demand, yet expenses had to be managed due to rising costs. In response to these pressures, management made a decision to change its policy of not requiring overtime in the summer. Temporary employees would be used where possible to minimize the impact to vacations plans, but the company had to hold the line on expenses. Therefore, some overtime would result and some vacations would be cut short. Supervisors had to tell employees of this switch in policy just before the summer vacation season started.

One supervisor held a brief meeting and told employees of the policy change. She explained she didn't like it but she had to follow it. So, she said didn't want any whining and presented the new schedule.

Another supervisor held a meeting and explained the change in policy. He empathized and listened to the employees' concerns. He gave details on why the company made the decision. He led the group in brainstorming how to implement the decision as fairly as possible. He acknowledged the late notice and recognized people for their contributions to their plan.

Which employee group do you suppose handled the change better? Obviously it was the second group. Why? The supervisor communicated change effectively. On the next page are some guidelines to help.

Ten Commandments for Implementing Change

1. Communicate specifics early and follow-up information regularly

2. Include others ideas for the change if possible

3. Describe changes in as much detail as you can

4. Offer training to help with new skills or to overcome obstacles

5. Listen to and acknowledge people's feelings and concerns

6. Get all people involved in some way to be accountable for the success of the change

7. Brainstorm and focus on the "possibilities" of change

8. Facilitate creative problem solving and planning

9. Pay particular attention to those who have a difficult time with change

10. Recognize and reward progress in implementation

Techniques for Communicating Change

In all change, communicate beforehand, communicate during execution, and communicate about results. You need to do this in the following ways. The first two points were described in earlier chapters. The next three will be outlined in the coming pages.

➤ Hold department meetings

➤ Conduct one-on-one sessions

➤ Use change-management skills

➤ Get people involved through brainstorming

➤ Do group problem solving

Change-Management Skills

During times of change you need to be aware of how individuals perform and also how everyone works together. You need to communicate more, not less, during times of change. In Part 3: Communicating with Others, you were introduced to the acronym TEAM Communication. It is a key to effective change management. TEAM also refers to strategies for managing change:

Together focus on a purpose of the change.

Empower others to participate positively in adjusting to the change.

Aim for consensus on how to achieve the goals of the change.

Manage the process to track more effective results.

The chart on the next page explains these strategies in more detail. Use it as a checkpoint to gauge the team efforts of your employees and determine what actions you can take to help them through the change. Highlight or underline key ideas as you review it.

CHANGE-MANAGEMENT SKILLS

TEAM PROCESS	EMPLOYEE NEEDS	SUPERVISOR BEHAVIOR	EMPLOYEE BEHAVIOR
Together focus on a purpose	• Common goals • Attention to content • Leadership support	• Interpret company goals • Facilitate team's establishment of and buy-in to goals • Evaluate and track progress toward goals • Hold department meetings and one-on-one sessions	• Clarify boundaries • Ask questions to test own understanding • Participate in making things better • Help leader track and evaluate progress toward goals
Empower others to participate	• High level of involvement/communication • Empathy • Maintenance of self-esteem • Leadership support • Respect for differences • Trust	• Ask questions • Listen to concerns/resistance • Show understanding • Summarize feelings about the situation • Encourage people to move forward • Encourage and support others	• Contribute ideas • Build on others' ideas • Consider others' ideas • Think creatively
Aim for consensus	• Constructive conflict resolution • Power within group to be involved in decisions • Leadership support • Trust • Pride and self-satisfaction	• Use group-process techniques (brainstorm, problem solving) • Ask questions • Listen • Seek common interests • Summarize • Confront in constructive way	• Focus on common interests and goals • Encourage others to talk • Listen to and consider others' ideas • Make own needs known • Disagree in a constructive way • Summarize points
Manage the process	• Attention to process • Leadership support • Trust • Recognition	• Give clear directions • Intervene to keep everyone on track • Read group and adjust • Be positive • Suggest alternative • Communicate results • Provide training	• Listen • Keep purpose • Stay focused on objective • Use own energy and enthusiasm to help process along • Perform well

Brainstorming Change Ideas

An effective tool for gaining employee input, buy-in, and involvement in a change or an improvement process is brainstorming. Brainstorming means you ask others to share ideas related to a task, goal, or change.

Guidelines for Brainstorming

➤ Go for quantity rather than quality, to keep ideas flowing

➤ Absolutely no criticism is allowed

➤ Everyone's participation is encouraged

 – Give people a few minutes to write individual notes

 – Share one idea at a time through a round robin or two

➤ Build on each other's ideas

➤ Move quickly

➤ Creative or weird ideas are helpful

The Brainstorming Process

1. Set a predetermined time limit for sharing (5–15 minutes).

2. Pose a question such as: How can we implement this change positively?

3. Write all ideas on a flip chart or whiteboard (use the speaker's words).

4. Read the list of ideas.

5. Ask, what can we learn from this exercise?

6. Ask everyone to identify individually the top five to seven ideas.

7. Record votes for each idea. Identify the top ideas.

8. Review ways to implement various ideas.

9. Create plans to follow through.

Uses of Brainstorming

Brainstorming can be used in other ways also. Here is a list; put a check (✔) next to one area you can apply it to, or add your own area.

❏ Improve a procedure

❏ Increase quality/service

❏ Build teamwork

❏ Increase productivity

❏ Other:_____

Problem-Solving Techniques

Someone once said, "The more problems you have the more alive you are." Without problems there would be no need for supervisors. When confronted with problems you need a problem-solving process.

The Problem-Solving Process

1. Clearly and specifically identify the problem.

2. Outline three to five obstacles that get in the way of success.

3. Outline three to five forces that will help your success.

4. Identify three alternative solutions and the possible outcomes.

5. Decide on a course of action. (You may need to explore the other solutions later.)

6. Create a specific plan to implement the solution. Add timelines.

A sales supervisor had a new product to sell. After a couple of weeks results were poor. Because of the fast rollout of the product, minimal training was provided beforehand. After listening to some calls and talking to her reps, the supervisor used the problem-solving process to deal with the issue. Reps were divided into three groups to receive three short training sessions over a two-week period. The training focused on product knowledge and handling objections. Results improved dramatically.

PROBLEM-SOLVING PRACTICE

Identify a problem you are facing and use the Problem-Solving Process on the previous page as a guide to help you improve. Whether you are faced with change or not, this process can help you keep a positive attitude. In this era of fast-paced change, if you aren't getting better, you are getting worse. Always have goals and plans to move forward.

Problem Statement:

Obstacles:

Support:

Alternative Solutions:

A.

B.

C.

Recommended solution:

Action Steps

A.

B.

C.

CASE STUDY 5

Read the case situations below and circle which change strategy the supervisors should use with employees to help deal with the process. Check (✔) all that apply.

1. Business has been great for five years at a delivery company. Recently it slowed down considerably. The company was concerned. How could a marketing supervisor help?

   ❑ Department meeting   ❑ One-on-ones

   ❑ Brainstorming   ❑ Problem solving

2. A high-tech company in a large metropolitan area was expanding rapidly through acquisitions. As new products came on line the order department always had system problems to deal with. How could the supervisor handle this difficult situation?

   ❑ Department meeting   ❑ One-on-ones

   ❑ Brainstorming   ❑ Problem solving

3. A car dealership was receiving numerous complaints and poor survey ratings about its cars' cleanliness upon delivery. How could the vehicle-prep supervisor work through his employees to improve?

   ❑ Department meeting   ❑ One-on-ones

   ❑ Brainstorming   ❑ Problem solving

4. A manufacturing company completed an employee-attitude survey. The production department's ratings indicated negative attitudes from employees about the areas of communication and leadership. The production manager held a meeting with the supervisors to review results. What do the supervisors need to do?

    ❑ Department meeting   ❑ One-on-ones

    ❑ Brainstorming   ❑ Problem solving

5. A marketing company significantly changed its incentive plan for customers to counteract competition. While customer feedback was great, response time to customer calls and requests became unacceptably slow. How should the customer-service manager respond?

    ❑ Department meeting   ❑ One-on-ones

    ❑ Brainstorming   ❑ Problem solving

6. A national industrial company was experiencing new and intense competition in a market it dominated. In an effort to keep business, local offices implemented a customer-loyalty campaign. Area supervisors were charged with improving the sales and service of all service representatives. How should the supervisors follow through?

    ❑ Department meeting   ❑ One-on-ones

    ❑ Brainstorming   ❑ Problem solving

Compare your responses to the author's suggestions in the back of the book.

Strategies for Managing Change

Review the strategies for managing change and put a check (✔) next to the ones you will try and add these to your action plans.

❑ **Communicate changes positively.** As a supervisor, you won't always be on the front end of organizational changes. Your job will often be to implement changes. Sometimes it won't be pleasant because it may mean procedural changes, downsizing, layoffs, or cost controls. However, you can always communicate and demonstrate empathy. Use meetings and one-on-one sessions to gain ideas or allow people to vent feelings.

The Ten Commandments for Implementing Change remind you of how to make transitions more smoothly in your area. While upper management may not always do this, you can! What two or three of the commandments do you feel you can do well? What two or three commandments do you need to remember to do better? Are you in the midst of change now? Which commandments do you need to practice?

❑ **Apply change-management skills.** The TEAM chart shows you the behaviors you need to demonstrate, the needs of employees, and the involvement you want from employees. Where can you apply this today?

❑ **Conduct a brainstorming session.** Follow the process and follow up to use the ideas. Whether you are in the midst of massive change or not, use these techniques to gain employee ideas and commitment to improve results. Remember, most employees today want to feel a part of something—a team, cause, or purpose. You need their heads and hands, but also their hearts.

❑ **Implement the problem-solving process.** In Part 1: Getting Started, you created an action plan to prepare to win. How have things gone for you? What has worked well? What hasn't worked well? What will you do better or differently? Chances are you have some problems to solve. What's your biggest problem? Or, if things are going really well, where can you apply the continuous-improvement approach? Use it and you'll make more progress.

S U M M A R Y

" *Nothing in the world can take the place of persistence."*

—Calvin Coolidge

ACTION PLAN: KEEP EXCELLING

Listed below are all the suggested strategies in the book. Put a check (✔) next to the items you have accomplished. Then, consider which additional strategies you'd like to focus on next; place an (✘) next to those items. As you answer the questions that follow, make plans to incorporate these strategies into your Action Steps to help you achieve your goals.

Getting Started

- ❏ Obtain a copy of your job description (or create one)
- ❏ Talk to and interview three other supervisors or managers
- ❏ Make a plan to complete this book thoroughly
- ❏ Develop a written plan for your work area
- ❏ Meet with your boss

Managing for High Performance

- ❏ Hold a meeting with your employees
- ❏ Meet with each employee one-on-one
- ❏ Be available to employees
- ❏ Work cooperatively with others
- ❏ Make necessary changes

Communicating with Others Proactively

- ❏ Make a commitment to keep learning
- ❏ Prepare, prepare, prepare
- ❏ Ask for feedback
- ❏ Delegate tasks effectively
- ❏ Read a communication book

Action Plan: Keep Excelling (CONTINUED)

Coaching for Excellence

- ❑ Discuss the results of the Coaching for Excellence Inventory with your boss
- ❑ Review how you have applied informal coaching
- ❑ Complete a formal coaching with an employee
- ❑ Reward yourself

Dealing with Change Positively

- ❑ Communicate changes positively
- ❑ Apply change-management skills
- ❑ Conduct a brainstorming session
- ❑ Implement the problem-solving process

Overall, what have you done well as a supervisor?_____

_____

_____

Overall, what hasn't worked very well for you?_____

_____

_____

What do you need to improve and do better as you look ahead?_____

_____

_____

Department Goals/Priorities

1. _____
2. _____
3. _____
4. _____
5. _____

Based on the goals and priorities above, what actions will you take and what is your timeline for completing them?

Action Steps for Excellence	Timeline
1.	
2.	
3.	
4.	
5.	

Final Thoughts: How Good Can You Be?

How good can you be? Scientists estimate that the average human being uses less than 10% of his or her potential. Unfortunately, too many supervisors use excuses like:

➤ I don't have time

➤ Management doesn't support me

➤ Employees don't care

➤ Unions are too combative

➤ Customers don't understand

➤ I tried

On and on the whine list goes. But supervisors would be wise to remember that U.S. President Harry S. Truman's words, "The buck stops here," applies to all leaders. When you are a supervisor, you are accountable and responsible. There will be obstacles, some are very difficult, but few are really impossible to overcome.

Think of the Potential, Not the Problems

Cliff Miedl was a 20-year-old plumber's apprentice. While working on a job, he accidentally drove his jackhammer through three high-voltage cables. His body instantly received 30,000 volts of electricity. That's 15 times the amount people receive in the electric chair. The jolt blew off most his toes, shattered his knees, exploded part of his skull, and put a hole in his back as the electricity left his body. His heart stopped beating three times, yet he survived. Doctors said he'd never walk again.

Through a slow and painful recovery, he learned to walk again. Not only that—he was inspired by 1988 kayak Olympian Greg Barton (who had club feet) who won two gold medals in Seoul. So Miedl learned how to kayak. He became good at it and made the United States Olympic team. On opening night of the 2000 Sydney Games, the 603 members of the team voted him the flag bearer for their march into the stadium. Meidl turned a tragedy into a triumph.

Receiving 30,000 volts of electricity is hard. The road back is hard. Absent employees or management policy changes can be difficult to deal with but not hard compared to Meidl's ordeal. So always believe in the potential—what you can do or control. Don't waste time on what you can't do or can't control.

Be Action Oriented, Not Apathetic

Supervisors are the single biggest influence on employees' performance, according to Gallup Poll research. What an opportunity to make a difference! Too many supervisors give up, react negatively, or let events push them around. By taking action, you get things done.

A sports magazine ran an article about a man in the *Guinness Book of World Records* who ran 90 marathons in one year. In honor of the new millennium, he decided to run 200 marathons in 2000! When asked why, he replied he didn't want anyone to break his record, and he knew he could do it. What an attitude, and he acted on it! You don't need to run marathons unless you want to. As a supervisor, with the right actions—communication, goal setting, recognition, coaching, and problem solving—you can motivate others toward superb results.

Stay Proactive, Not Reactive

It's been said, "All great achievers are great planners." You have to have a plan and then adjust the plan as needed. Scientists say the difference between a human being and a gorilla in terms of DNA is 2.8%. It's not much, but it matters. The key ingredient there is humans' ability to think.

The objective of the Human Genome Project is to identify the human DNA map, cell by cell. The significance of this project is that it changes medicine from a reactive discipline to a proactive one. Scientists predict that if they can discover that a baby has a predisposition for disease before it is born, doctors could switch the cells to be preventive. While there are many ethical concerns to debate about this, the fact remains that human intellect has discovered the technology to make it possible.

Again, this demonstrates the capacity of a person to identify and solve problems. That's an important part of a supervisor's job. The next step is to work with employees to achieve the goal. Never underestimate the ability of people to excel or your ability to succeed.

Author's Notes on the Case Studies

Case Study 1 (page 14)

1. **What did supervisors do that are examples of poorly working through others?**

   ➤ Ruled with iron first—too authoritative

   ➤ Criticized an employee regularly

   ➤ Never tried anything new

   ➤ Played it safe—no risks

   ➤ Displayed know-it-all attitude

   ➤ Didn't support employees

   ➤ Lack of empathy for personal matters

   ➤ Lacked goals and direction

   ➤ Did not provide recognition

2. **The above nine areas are common mistakes for new supervisors.** Employees often respond negatively to this kind of treatment and they may complain more, make more mistakes, miss more work, decrease their performance and results, and serve customers less effectively.

3. **While learnings in these areas will vary, there are key points to keep in mind:**

   ➤ A supervisor's success depends on employees' success. Take the responsibility seriously.

   ➤ The best supervisors are people-oriented. They work hard to create a positive environment.

   ➤ The transition to supervisor is important. Focus on the people and results; don't be a dictator or a know-it-all in the process.

   ➤ The best supervisors leave clues to success. That's what *Excellence in Supervision* will give you.

   ➤ Finally, take action. Commit to learn all you can from the book. Read it your first week, month, and at six months. Commit to be the best you can be.

Case Study 2 (page 40)

1. Which employee do you think would make the transition to team leader most successfully? Why?

First of all, all three employees could succeed as a team leader. With the proper coaching and training, the potential is there for each person. However, of the three, Maria Sanchez has a better opportunity to succeed. Her performance is good, she has trained others, and she is willing to work hard.

2. What are reasons you didn't choose the others?

Joe has the technical skills and tenure. He does lack people skills and he is a loner. It may be too much of a challenge for him to get things done through others.

John gets along well with everyone and is also an effective employee. He may lack the willingness to work hard. He may also face too many challenges being a buddy of many of the employees.

Case Study 3 (page 58)

1. What are your reactions to how this delegation happened?

Cindy rushed the delegation and short-circuited the communication. Jim didn't get his questions or needs taken care of.

2. What should Cindy do to follow up?

She should see Jim as soon as possible and apologize for being abrupt. Then she should outline her expectations and a timeline for review, and answer any questions Jim may have.

3. What should Cindy do better or differently next time?

First, change her attitude about delegation. The goal is also to help develop employees, not to just off-load some work. Second, outline clear expectations, timelines, and rationale for the delegation. Third, answer any questions or concerns of the employee. Fourth, reassure the employee that he or she can do it. Fifth, make sure to follow up.

Case Study 4 (page 76)

1. How do you think Doug felt about his first day?

Doug probably felt more comfortable and relaxed. His boss, Kelli, talked to him at breakfast, introduced him to others, explained his job and goals, and took him to personnel.

What has been your experience in this type of situation?

This will vary per person. Hopefully, the experiences have been positive. My experiences have been a mixed bag, some good and others not.

How do you plan to handle an employee's first day?

To help new employees get off on the right foot, use the suggestions in the case. It's also a good idea to meet with the employee at the end of the first week and first month. During those meetings, discuss the job, progress made, and any questions or concerns of the employee.

2. Why do you think Ross reacted this way?

Ross and Pat are just getting to know each other. Ross is defensive and resistant to a new boss. He may not be used to one-on-ones or coaching. He may even have wanted to be the supervisor.

How do you engage someone who isn't very talkative in a meeting?

Whether in a one-on-one or in a group meeting, supervisors need to maintain the self-esteem and self-respect of employees. Don't be critical or judgmental. In a meeting, ask for their ideas politely. Ask people to write their ideas on paper and share them. Pair people up to talk and then ask for comments. In a one-on-one, ask for input politely, allow some silence, clarify your question, empathize with their concerns or feelings, and be patient. Over time, most people will open up; however, some people are shy or lower key and that's okay.

What should Pat do?

He needs to continue the sessions over time. He can try some of the one-in-one ideas mentioned above. If Ross doesn't open up, he will need to try the counseling method mentioned in Managing for High Performance.

Case Study 5 (pages 94–95)

1. As a first step, the supervisor could hold a department meeting to explain what's going on with the company. Then do some brainstorming to identify new, creative ideas to attract new customers. Later, problem solving and one-on-ones could be used for follow-up.

- ✓ Department meeting
- ✓ One-on-ones
- ✓ Brainstorming
- ✓ Problem solving

2. It sounds like new products consistently generated system problems. Including some employees in problem solving could result in a new process.

- ❏ Department meeting
- ❏ One-on-ones
- ❏ Brainstorming
- ✓ Problem solving

3. Many car dealerships experience this. At a department meeting, the supervisor could share survey results and listen to employee concerns. Then, form a team for problem solving and identify ways to improve. Finally, track results through the survey.

- ✓ Department meeting
- ❏ One-on-ones
- ❏ Brainstorming
- ✓ Problem solving

4. The production manager held a department meeting; all the supervisors could do the same in their areas and review the results of the attitude survey. As follow-up, the supervisors could do one-on-ones with employees. Also, if they applied the concepts of this book, attitudes would improve.

- ✓ Department meeting
- ✓ One-on-ones
- ❏ Brainstorming
- ❏ Problem solving

5. The supervisor could hold a department meeting and share the response time results; then brainstorm for ideas. Remember, this is a new process; the super-visor must realize there will be hiccups, so stay positive.

- ✓ Department meeting
- ❏ One-on-ones
- ✓ Brainstorming
- ❏ Problem solving

6. By gaining employee commitment and buy-in to the new campaign, the area supervisors could make great progress. Start with a department meeting to discuss the competition and new campaign. Next, brainstorm to identify two things: other ideas and ways to make the campaign work. Third, create one or more problem-solving groups to follow up the ideas. And do one-on-ones to review each employee's customers and needs.

✓	Department meeting	✓	One-on-ones
✓	Brainstorming	✓	Problem solving

NOTE: These four methods are tools to involve employees, communicate with them, and to help them deal with change. Be creative in how you apply them. The potential for positive progress is enormous.

Recommended Reading

Bonet, Diana. *The Business of Listening*. Menlo Park, CA: Crisp Publications, 2001.

Brounstein, Marty, and Beverly Manber. *Handling the Difficult Employee*. Menlo Park, CA: Crisp Publications, 1993.

Buckinghaj, Marus, and Curt Coffman. *First, Break All the Rules*. New York, NY: Simon Schuster, 1999.

Conlow, Rick. *Excellence in Management*. Menlo Park, CA: Crisp Publications, 2000.

Decker, Bert. *The Art of Communicating*. Menlo Park, CA: Crisp Publications, 1997.

Hathaway, Patti. *Giving and Receiving Feedback*. Menlo Park, CA: Crisp Publications, 1998.

Haynes, Marion E. *Effective Meeting Skills*. Menlo Park, CA: Crisp Publications, 1997.

Haynes, Marion E. *Personal Time Management*. Menlo Park, CA: Crisp Publications, 2000.

Johnson, Spencer. *Who Moved My Cheese?* New York, NY: G.P. Putnam's Sons, 1998.

Maddux, Robert. *Delegating for Results*. Menlo Park, CA: Crisp Publications, 1998.

Nelson, Bob. *1001 Ways to Reward Employees*. New York, NY: Workman Publishing Company, 1994.

Pokras, Sandy. *Team Problem Solving*. Menlo Park, CA: Crisp Publications, 1995.

Scott, Cynthia D., and Dennis T. Jaffe. *Empowerment*. Menlo Park, CA: Crisp Publications, 1991.

Scott, Cynthia D., and Dennis T. Jaffe. *Managing Change at Work*. Menlo Park, CA: Crisp Publications, 1995.

NOTES

Now Available From

CRISP. Learning™

Books•Videos•CD-ROMs•Computer-Based Training Products

If you enjoyed this book, we have great news for you.
There are over 200 books available in the *Fifty-Minute™ Series*.
To request a free full-line catalog, contact your local distributor or

Crisp Learning
1200 Hamilton Court
Menlo Park, CA 94025
1-800-442-7477
CrispLearning.com

Subject Areas Include:

Management
Human Resources
Communication Skills
Personal Development
Marketing/Sales
Organizational Development
Customer Service/Quality
Computer Skills
Small Business and Entrepreneurship
Adult Literacy and Learning
Life Planning and Retirement

Excellence in Supervision

CRISP WORLDWIDE DISTRIBUTION

English language books are distributed worldwide. Major international distributors include:

ASIA/PACIFIC

Australia/New Zealand: In Learning, PO Box 1051, Springwood QLD, Brisbane, Australia 4127   Tel: 61-7-3-841-2286, Facsimile: 61-7-3-841-1580
ATTN: Messrs. Richard/Robert Gordon

Malaysia, Philippines, Singapore: Epsys Pte Ltd., 540 Sims Ave #04-01, Sims Avenue Centre, 387603, Singapore   Tel: 65-747-1964, Facsimile: 65-747-0162 ATTN: Mr. Jack Chin

Hong Kong/Mainland China: Crisp Learning Solutions, 18/F Honest Motors Building 9-11 Leighton Rd., Causeway Bay, Hong Kong   Tel: 852-2915-7119, Facsimile: 852-2865-2815 ATTN: Ms. Grace Lee

Japan: Phoenix Associates, Believe Mita Bldg., 8th Floor 3-43-16 Shiba, Minato-ku, Tokyo 105-0014, Japan   Tel: 81-3-5427-6231, Facsimile: 81-3-5427-6232
ATTN: Mr. Peter Owans

CANADA

Crisp Learning Canada, 60 Briarwood Avenue, Mississauga, ON L5G 3N6 Canada
Tel: 905-274-5678, Facsimile: 905-278-2801
ATTN: Mr. Steve Connolly

EUROPEAN UNION

England: Flex Learning Media, Ltd., 9-15 Hitchin Street, Baldock, Hertfordshire, SG7 6AL, England
Tel: 44-1-46-289-6000, Facsimile: 44-1-46-289-2417   ATTN: Mr. David Willetts

INDIA

Multi-Media HRD, Pvt. Ltd., National House, Floor 1
6 Tulloch Road, Appolo Bunder, Bombay, India 400-039
Tel: 91-22-204-2281, Facsimile: 91-22-283-6478
ATTN: Messrs. Ajay Aggarwal/ C.L. Aggarwal

SOUTH AMERICA

Mexico: Grupo Editorial Iberoamerica, Nebraska 199, Col. Napoles, 03810 Mexico, D.F.
Tel: 525-523-0994, Facsimile: 525-543-1173   ATTN: Señor Nicholas Grepe

SOUTH AFRICA

Bookstores: Alternative Books, PO Box 1345, Ferndale 2160, South Africa
Tel: 27-11-792-7730, Facsimile: 27-11-792-7787   ATTN: Mr. Vernon de Haas

Corporate: Learning Resources, P.O. Box 2806, Parklands, Johannesburg 2121, South Africa, Tel: 27-21-531-2923, Facsimile: 27-21-531-2944 ATTN: Mr. Ricky Robinson

MIDDLE EAST

Edutech Middle East, L.L.C., PO Box 52334, Dubai U.A.E.
Tel: 971-4-359-1222, Facsimile: 971-4-359-6500   ATTN: Mr. A.S.F. Karim